**NATIONAL
GEOGRAPHIC**

Water Can Change

Brian Birchall

Contents

Ice

Ice is hard and cold.
Ice is a solid.

A solid has
its own shape.

3

What happens when you put ice in the sun?

1 **The heat from the sun melts the ice.**

œ

2 The hard ice changes.,

3 The ice becomes water.   5

Water

Water is a liquid. The heat changed the ice to water. The heat changed the solid to a liquid.

A liquid is runny. It flows easily. A liquid takes the shape of its container.

What happens when you heat water?

1 The heat makes the water boil.

2 The water changes.

3 The water becomes steam.

9

Steam

Steam is a gas. The heat changed the water to steam. The heat changed the liquid to a gas.

It is hard to see most gases. A gas goes into the air. A gas spreads to fill any space.

11

Heat can make things change.

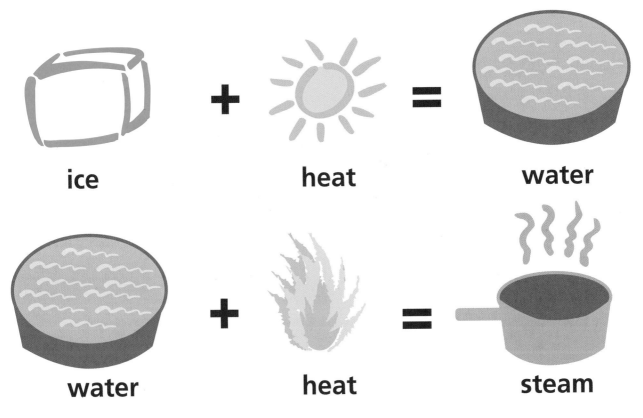

ice + heat = water

water + heat = steam